Beatrix Potter
99 Cliparts Book Part 3

15_Cliparts_Todd.png

by
Elizabeth M. Potter

Content	Page

99 Cliparts

Bibliografische Information der Deutschen Nationalbibliothek:
Die Deutsche Nationalbibliothek verzeichnet diese Publikation in der Deutschen Nationalbibliografie; detaillierte bibliografische
Daten sind im Internet über http://dnb.dnb.de abrufbar.

© 2018 Elizabeth M. Potter 1. Auflage
Covergrafik, Texte und Bilder: © 2018 Elizabeth M. Potter

Herstellung und Verlag: BoD – Books on Demand, Norderstedt

ISBN: 9783752867091

The Tale of Squirrel Nutkin

1_Clipart_Nutkin.png

2_Clipart_Nutkin.png

3_Clipart_Nutkin.png

4_Clipart_Nutkin.png

5_Clipart_Nutkin.png

6_Clipart_Nutkin.png

7_Clipart_Nutkin.png

8_Clipart_Nutkin.png

9_Clipart_Nutkin.png

10_Clipart_Nutkin.png

11_Clipart_Nutkin.png

12_Clipart_Nutkin.png

13_Clipart_Nutkin.png

14_Clipart_Nutkin.png

15_Clipart_Nutkin.png

16_Clipart_Nutkin.png

17_Clipart_Nutkin.png

18_Clipart_Nutkin.png

19_Clipart_Nutkin.png

20_Clipart_Nutkin.png

21_Clipart_Nutkin.png

22_Clipart_Nutkin.png

23_Clipart_Nutkin.png

The Tale of Two Bad Mice

1_Cliparts_bad_mice.png

2_Cliparts_bad_mice.png

3_Cliparts_bad_mice.png

4_Cliparts_bad_mice.png

5_Cliparts_bad_mice.png

6_Cliparts_bad_mice.png

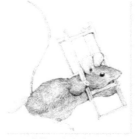

7_Cliparts_bad_mice.png

8_Cliparts_bad_mice.png

9_Cliparts_bad_mice.png

10_Cliparts_bad_mice.png

11_Cliparts_bad_mice.png

12_Cliparts_bad_mice.p

13_Cliparts_bad_mice.png

14_Cliparts_bad_mice.png

15_Cliparts_bad_mice.png

16_Cliparts_bad_mic

17_Cliparts_bad_mice.png

18_Cliparts_bad_mice.png

19_Cliparts_bad_mice.png

20_Cliparts_bad_mice.png

21_Cliparts_bad_mice.png

22_Cliparts_bad_mice.png

The Tale of Mrs. Tittlemouse

1_Cliparts_Mrs.Tittlemouse.png

2_Cliparts_Mrs.Tittlemouse.png

3_Cliparts_Mrs.Tittlemouse.png

4_Cliparts_Mrs.Tittlemouse.png

5_Cliparts_Mrs.Tittlemouse.png

6_Cliparts_Mrs.Tittlemouse.png

7_Cliparts_Mrs.Tittlemouse.png

8_Cliparts_Mrs.Tittlemouse.png

9_Cliparts_Mrs.Tittlemouse.png

10_Cliparts_Mrs.Tittlemouse.png

11_Cliparts_Mrs.Tittlemouse.png

12_Cliparts_Mrs.Tittlemouse.png

13_Cliparts_Mrs.Tittlemouse.png

14_Cliparts_Mrs.Tittlemouse.png

15_Cliparts_Mrs.Tittlemouse.png

16_Cliparts_Mrs.Tittlemouse.png

17_Cliparts_Mrs.Tittlemouse.png

18_Cliparts_Mrs.Tittlemouse.png

19_Cliparts_Mrs.Tittlemouse.png

20_Cliparts_Mrs.Tittlemouse.png

14

The Tale of Mr. Tod

1_Cliparts_Todd.png

2_Cliparts_Todd.png

3_Cliparts_Todd.png

4_Cliparts_Todd.png

5_Cliparts_Todd.png

6_Cliparts_Todd.png

7_Cliparts_Todd.png

8_Cliparts_Todd.png

9_Cliparts_Todd.png

10_Cliparts_Todd.png

11_Cliparts_Todd.png

12_Cliparts_Todd.png

13_Cliparts_Todd.png

14_Cliparts_Todd.png

15_Cliparts_Todd.png

16_Cliparts_Todd.png

17_Cliparts_Todd.png

18_Cliparts_Todd.png

19_Cliparts_Todd.png

20_Cliparts_Todd.png

The Tale of Johnny Town-Mouse

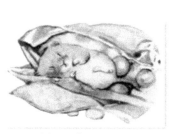

1_Cliparts_Townmouse.png

2_Cliparts_Townmouse.png

3_Cliparts_Townmouse.png

4_Cliparts_Townmouse.png

2nd Part of link: **AADbBjje_U1drPN2cqRUHPOca?dl=0**

5_Cliparts_Townmouse.png

6_Cliparts_Townmouse.png

7_Cliparts_Townmouse.png

8_Cliparts_Townmouse.png

9_Cliparts_Townmouse.png

10_Cliparts_Townmouse.png

11_Cliparts_Townmouse.png

12_Cliparts_Townmouse.png

13_Cliparts_Townmouse.png

14_Cliparts_Townmouse.png

15_Cliparts_Townmouse.png

Instructions for downloading the Cliparts

Before you are reading the instructions to download/using the cliparts, please read the following handling instructions for the correct usage of the cliparts.

Handling instruction for the usage of the cliparts

The cliparts were created by Elizabeth M. Potter. Therefore please take into account the following before starting the download:

You can use the cliparts for any of your private enterprises, projects, presentations, invitations or the like.
But it is not allowed to use them for commercial purpurses.
If you intend to use them for commercial purpurses, please ask for written approval by Elizabeth M. Potter in advance (elizabeth.potter@t-online.de).
In that case, publishing, republishing or reproductions of the cliparts, especially of the download link, via any kind of service, Internet or graphic service wether as a book, electronically, or via other not listed above media or other means, without prior approval by Elizabeth M. Potter is strongly prohibited.

- -

Clipart download instructions

The cliparts are in a directory of dropbox Service. It is a simple access by typing in the download link into your internet browser. The access is possible via PC, smartphone or tablet. The clipart files are presented in png-format.
For security reasons the link is divided into two parts. For gaining the complete link, both parts have to be typed into the address field of the browser one after another without spaces in between.

1st Part of link: **https://www.dropbox.com/sh/n1v9by685jrh0zu/**
2nd Part of link: you will find on page 19 of this book

Further books of Elizabeth M. Potter

NOTEBOOKS
The Peter Rabbit Notebook
PAINTING BOOKS
Beatrix Potter Painting Book Part 1 (Peter Rabbit)
Beatrix Potter Painting Book Part 2 (Peter Rabbit)
Beatrix Potter Painting Book Part 3 (Peter Rabbit)
Beatrix Potter Painting Book Part 4 (Peter Rabbit)
Beatrix Potter Painting Book Part 5 (Peter Rabbit)
Beatrix Potter Painting Book Part 6 (Peter Rabbit)
Beatrix Potter Painting Book Part 7 (Peter Rabbit)
Beatrix Potter Painting Book Part 8 (Peter Rabbit)
Beatrix Potter Painting Book Part 9 (Peter Rabbit)
Beatrix Potter Painting Book Part 10 (Peter Rabbit)
Peter Rabbit Painting Book
CLIPART BOOKS
Beatrix Potter 99 Cliparts Book Part 1 (Peter Rabbit)
Beatrix Potter 99 Cliparts Book Part 2 (Peter Rabbit)
Beatrix Potter 99 Cliparts Book Part 3 (Peter Rabbit)
Beatrix Potter 99 Cliparts Book Part 4 (Peter Rabbit)
PASSWORD BOOKS
The Peter Rabbit Passwortbook